HIGH-BEGINNING

# Health Stories

## Readings and Language Activities for Healthy Choices

Ann Gianola

Instructor, San Diego Community College District
Instructor, University of San Diego English Language Academy
San Diego, California

**New Readers Press**

D0521004

Health Stories: Readings and Language Activities for Healthy Choices
High Beginning
ISBN 978-1-56420-702-9

Copyright © 2007 New Readers Press
New Readers Press
Division of ProLiteracy Worldwide
1320 Jamesville Avenue, Syracuse, New York 13210
www.newreaderspress.com

Printed in the United States of America
9  8  7  6  5  4  3  2  1

All proceeds from the sale of New Readers Press materials
support literacy programs in the United States and worldwide.

**Developmental Editor:** Paula L. Schlusberg
**Creative Director:** Andrea Woodbury
**Illustrations:** Seitu Hayden and Roger Audette, Represented by Wilkinson Studios Inc.
**Production Specialist:** Maryellen Casey

# Contents

# LESSON 1

## Fast Food Decision

Oscar goes out for lunch almost every day. He eats a lot of fast food. Right now Oscar is looking at the big signs along the street. He is trying to make a decision. "Do I want a cheeseburger, pizza, fried chicken, a taco, or a hot dog?" he thinks. Then Oscar sees Patrick, his co-worker.

"Don't do it," says Patrick. "It's bad for you."

"Do what?" asks Oscar.

"Don't eat in those fast food restaurants," says Patrick. "There are more than 500 **calories** in a quarter-pound cheeseburger. There are 25 **fat grams.**" Then Patrick invites Oscar to go with him to the Greenhouse Café. He tells Oscar the restaurant serves very **healthy** food. Oscar sighs. He isn't very excited.

Oscar and Patrick walk into the restaurant. Patrick orders vegetable soup and fresh fruit. Oscar orders a spinach salad and whole-grain bread. Their food is delicious. "I feel good," says Oscar. "This food isn't heavy or greasy."

"And it is low in calories and fat grams," says Patrick.

"Yes, let's eat here again." Oscar looks at his watch and stands up. "But I'm in a hurry now. I want to pick up an extra-large double-chocolate shake at the fast food place."

## Answer the questions.

1. How often does Oscar go out to lunch?

2. What does he eat a lot of?

3. Who is Patrick?

4. What does Patrick say about fast food?

5. How many calories are in a quarter-pound cheeseburger?

6. How many fat grams are in a quarter-pound cheeseburger?

7. Where does Patrick invite Oscar to go?

8. What does Oscar order?

9. How is their food?

10. What does Oscar want to pick up after lunch?

# Which category is it?

| | | | |
|---|---|---|---|
| calories | cholesterol | fried chicken | heavy |
| carbohydrates | delicious | greasy | hot dog |
| cheeseburger | fat grams | healthy | pizza |

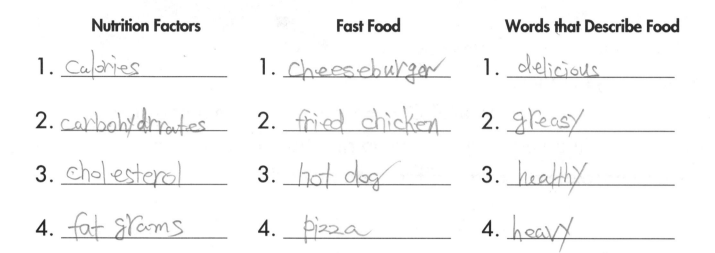

| Nutrition Factors | Fast Food | Words that Describe Food |
|---|---|---|
| 1. Calories | 1. Cheeseburger | 1. delicious |
| 2. carbohydrates | 2. fried chicken | 2. greasy |
| 3. cholesterol | 3. hot dog | 3. healthy |
| 4. fat grams | 4. pizza | 4. heavy |

## Matching: Definitions

_f_ 1. healthy    a. food that is served quickly

_b_ 2. gram    b. a unit of weight used to measure fat in a food

_a_ 3. fast food    c. a choice you make

_e_ 4. greasy    d. units that measure the energy a food produces

_c_ 5. decision    e. oily or fatty

_d_ 6. calories    f. good for you

## Talking to the Doctor

Practice the dialog with a partner.

How is your diet?

**Well, I eat a lot of fast food.**

How often do you eat it?

**I eat it almost every day for lunch.**

That's a lot of calories and fat grams.

**I know. I need to think about what I eat.**

## Fast Food Menu

Look at the information about some of the fast food Oscar eats. Then answer the questions.

|  | **Calories** | **Fat Grams** |
| --- | --- | --- |
| Quarter-pound cheeseburger | 510 | 25 |
| Large slice of pizza | 730 | 37 |
| Fried chicken plate | 560 | 31 |
| Giant hot dog with ketchup | 455 | 14 |
| Large taco meal | 450 | 21 |
| Double-chocolate shake | 580 | 14 |

1. How many fat grams does the pizza have? _____ 37 _____

2. How many calories does the large taco meal have? __ 450 ___

3. Which food has 510 calories? _Quarter-pound cheeseburger_

4. Which food has the most calories? _Large of pizza_

5. Which food has the most fat grams? _S Large of pizza_

## Sequence the story.

**Put the sentences in the order of the story. Number from 1 to 6.**

_4_ Patrick invites Oscar to the Greenhouse Café.

_6_ Oscar wants the extra-large double-chocolate shake.

_2_ Then Oscar sees Patrick, his co-worker.

_5_ Oscar orders a spinach salad and whole-grain bread.

_1_ Oscar looks at the big signs along the street.

_3_ Patrick says, "Don't do it. It's bad for you."

## Problem Solving

I eat a lot of fast food. I want to eat a lunch with fewer calories and fat grams. What can I do? Check the good ideas. Write other good ideas on the lines.

✓ I can pack a healthy lunch at home.

✗ I can choose the healthy items at a fast food restaurant.

✗ I can eat a hamburger instead of a cheeseburger.

✓ I can check menu items for calories and fat grams.

✗ I can stop eating lunch and have fast food for dinner.

✓ I can  cook by my self x

✓ I can  choose good health restaurant

# What about you?

Check *Yes* or *No*. Then write the questions and ask your partner.

**Yes    No**

___✓___  ___✓___  1. I go out to lunch almost every day.

**Do you go out to lunch almost every day?**

___✓___  _____  2. I think fast food is bad for you.

_____

_____  ___✓___  3. I think about calories when I eat something.

_____

_____  ___✓___  4. I think about fat grams when I eat something.

_____

___✓___  _____  5. I try not to eat food that is heavy or greasy.

_____

## Topics for Discussion or Writing

1. Do you eat fast food? If so, how often? Where do you usually go?

2. Where are some places in your community that serve healthy food?

3. Why do you think that so many people eat fast food?

Hello, Dr. Wilkins.

## LESSON 2

### Allergic to Penicillin

Sami is taking **penicillin** for **strep throat.** After four days, he is feeling better. But this morning Sami sees a terrible **rash** on his body. He has large red spots all over his back, chest, arms, and stomach. Sami is worried and calls the doctor. The doctor tells him to come in right away. He also tells him to stop taking the penicillin.

The doctor looks carefully at Sami's rash in the examining room. He asks Sami many questions. "These spots on your body are **hives,**" says the doctor. "You are **allergic** to penicillin."

"But I need to take penicillin for six more days," says Sami. "Strep throat is serious."

"There are many **antibiotics,**" says the doctor. "I can write a **prescription** for another one." The doctor also recommends an **antihistamine** for Sami's hives.

"A **penicillin allergy** is important information," says the doctor. "Always tell doctors and other medical professionals." He also tells Sami to carry a **medical alert card** in his wallet. "A penicillin allergy can be **life-threatening.**"

"OK," says Sami. "I can do that." Sami leaves the doctor's office. He gets in his car and drives up to the parking attendant.

"Have a nice day," says the parking attendant.

"You too," says Sami. "And don't forget. I am allergic to penicillin."

## Answer the questions.

1. Why is Sami taking penicillin?

2. Where does he see large red spots?

3. When does the doctor tell him to come in?

4. What does the doctor tell him to stop?

5. What are the spots on his body?

6. Why does he have the spots?

7. How many more days does Sami need an antibiotic?

8. What can the doctor write a prescription for?

9. What does the doctor recommend for Sami's hives?

10. What is important information?

# Check the sentence that means the same.

1. This morning Sami sees a terrible rash on his body.

   ___✓___ a. Sami has large red spots all over his back, chest, arms, and stomach.

   _____ b. Sami has a few red spots on his back.

2. The doctor tells him to come in right now.

   _____ a. The doctor tells him to come in tomorrow.

   ___✓___ b. The doctor tells him to come in immediately.

3. The doctor tells him to stop taking the penicillin.

   _____ a. Sami cannot take penicillin after six more days.

   ___✓___ b. Sami cannot take any more penicillin.

4. You are allergic to penicillin.

   _____ a. You need this antibiotic for strep throat.

   ___✓___ b. This antibiotic gives you a bad physical reaction.

5. Always tell doctors and other medical professionals.

   ___✓___ a. Give this information to people who treat you.

   _____ b. This is personal. Don't talk about it with anyone.

6. A penicillin allergy can be life-threatening.

   ___✓___ a. You can die if you have penicillin.

   _____ b. You need penicillin all your life.

## Talking to the Doctor

**Practice the dialog with a partner.**

I'm worried. I have this rash all over.

**Those are hives. Are you still taking the penicillin?**

Yes. I need to take it for six more days.

**Stop taking it. You are allergic to it.**

But I have strep throat. Isn't that serious?

**Yes. But I can write a prescription for another antibiotic. And an antihistamine can help the hives go away.**

## Medical Alert Card

**Read the alert card in Sami's wallet. Then answer the questions.**

---

### MEDICAL ALERT CARD

**Sami Mansour**     *Phone:* (213) 555-3749
1947 Vista Grande Avenue
Los Angeles, California  90047

*Physician:*
Mark Wilkins     *Phone:* (213) 555-0816

*Allergies:* Penicillin          *Blood Type:* O+

---

1. What is Sami's last name?  *Mansour*

2. What is his address?  *1947 Vista Grande Avenue Los Angeles, California 90047*

3. Who is his physician?  *Mark Wilkins*

4. What is Sami allergic to?  *Penicillin*

5. What is his blood type?  *O+ = positive*

# Sequence the pictures.

**Listen. Then number the pictures in the correct order.**

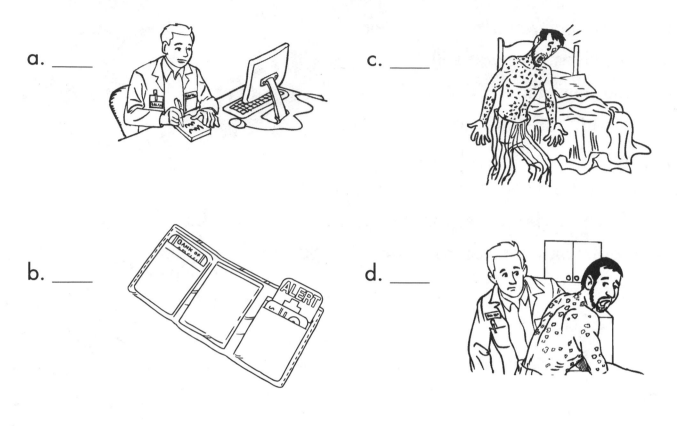

a. ____

c. ____

b. ____

d. ____

# Problem Solving

You have a medication allergy that can be life-threatening. What can you do? Check the good ideas. Write other good ideas on the lines.

____ I can keep it a secret.      ✓ I can tell the dentist.

____ I can tell the parking attendant.      ✓ I can tell a new doctor.

✓ I can carry an alert card in my wallet.

____ I can take a little of the medication.

✓ I can wear an alert bracelet or necklace.

✓ I can _____      ✓ I can _____

# What about you?

Check *Yes* or *No*. Then write the questions and ask your partner.

**Yes**   **No**

___ ✓  1. I sometimes get strep throat.

✓  <u>**Do you sometimes get strep throat?**</u>

✓ ___  2. I sometimes get worried and call the doctor.

_____

___ ✓  3. I take penicillin when I need to.

_____

✓ ___  4. I take other antibiotics when I need to.

_____

✓ ___  5. I tell medical professionals important information.

_____

## Topics for Discussion or Writing

1. What things can cause an allergic reaction?

2. What symptoms can you get if you have an allergic reaction?

3. Why is it important to tell medical professionals about a medication allergy?

# LESSON 3

## Losing Weight

Rico is 40 years old. He now weighs 50 **pounds** more than he did in high school. Rico doesn't look **healthy,** and he doesn't feel healthy. He has no **energy.** He gets **out of breath** easily.

Rico goes to the doctor's office for a complete **physical exam.** The doctor advises Rico to lose weight. "People who are **overweight** have more serious health problems," says the doctor. "You increase your risk of **heart disease.**" She talks about **type 2 diabetes.** She talks about high **cholesterol** and high **blood pressure.** The doctor gives Rico some suggestions about **diet** and **exercise.** "Lose weight slowly and sensibly," she says. "You can't lose 50 pounds overnight."

Rico often thinks about his doctor's advice. He walks daily for exercise. He uses the stairs whenever he can. He eats a **balanced diet.** He doesn't fry his food anymore. He bakes, broils, and steams when he cooks.

Rico returns to the doctor after nine months. He is 50 pounds lighter. He looks healthy and feels healthy. "Congratulations," says the doctor. "Now study hard and go to college."

"Doctor," says Rico. "I am not a student. I am 40 years old."

"Yes," says the doctor. "But you look like you are in high school."

## Answer the questions.

1. How old is Rico?

2. How many more pounds does he weigh now than he weighed in high school?

3. How does Rico look and feel?

4. What does the doctor advise Rico to do?

5. What health problems can people who are overweight have?

6. How does the doctor want Rico to lose weight?

7. What does Rico do to lose weight?

8. How does Rico cook his food?

9. When does Rico return to the doctor?

10. How much lighter is he?

# Which category is it?

| | | | |
|---|---|---|---|
| bake | climbing stairs | high blood pressure | swimming |
| biking | fry | high cholesterol | type 2 diabetes |
| broil | heart disease | steam | walking |

### Health Problems
1. heart disease
2. high blood pressure
3. high cholesterol
4. type 2 diabetes

### Ways to Cook
1. bake  steam
2. fry  broil
3. _____
4. _____

### Exercise
1. biking
2. Swimming
3. Walking
4. climbing stairs

# Matching: Opposites

_f_ 1. lose

_a_ 2. increase

_b_ 3. high

_a_ 4. slowly

_d_ 5. lighter

_g_ 6. sensibly

_e_ 7. serious

✓ a. quickly

✓ b. low

✓ c. decrease

✓ d. heavier

✓ e. unimportant

f. gain

✓ g. foolishly

## Talking to the Doctor

**Practice the dialog with a partner.**

You weigh 240 pounds.

**Oh, no. I'm 50 pounds heavier than I was in high school.**

You need to lose weight.

**I know. I have no energy and I get out of breath easily.**

And you're increasing your risk of many serious health problems.

**Do you have any suggestions for me?**

Read this information. Lose weight slowly and sensibly.

## Healthy Cooking

**Read the information the doctor gave Rico. Then answer the questions.**

> Healthy cooking can help you lose weight. Bake, broil, grill, and steam when you cook. You keep in flavor and nutrients and leave out extra fat and sodium. Never fry food in oil or butter. In sauces, use fruit juice or vegetable juice instead of oil and other fats. Non-stick cooking sprays can also reduce the fat and calories in your meals.

1. What can healthy cooking help you do? *Help you lose weight. Bake, broil grill and steam*

2. What do you keep in when you bake, broil, grill, and steam? *keep in flavor and nutrients and leave out*

3. What do you leave out? *leave out extra fat and sodium*

4. What can you use in sauces? *Use fruit juice or vegetable juice instead*

5. What do non-stick cooking sprays do? *Can also reduce the fat and calories in meals*

# Write the number of pounds you hear.

1. 2890

2. 118

3. 545

4. 1200

5. 259

6. _____

7. _____

8. _____

9. _____

10. _____

## Problem Solving

You want to lose 50 pounds to look healthy and feel healthy. What can you do? Check the good ideas. Write other good ideas on the lines.

No I can try to lose all 50 pounds in two months.

Yes I can walk daily for exercise.

_____ I can use elevators and escalators instead of stairs.

No I can fry food in oil and butter.

Yes I can go to the doctor's office for a complete physical exam.

Yes I can lose weight slowly and sensibly.

Yes I can bake, broil, grill, and steam when I cook.

✓ I can _____

✓ I can _____

## What about you?

Check *Yes* or *No*. Then write the questions and ask your partner.

**Yes**  **No**

✓  ____  1. I look and feel healthy.

_Do you look and feel healthy?_ _____

Yes  ____  2. I know about heart disease and type 2 diabetes.

_____

Yes  ____  3. I know about high cholesterol and high blood pressure.

_____

Yes  ____  4. I think it's important to lose weight slowly and sensibly.

_____

Yes  ____  5. I exercise daily.

_____

## Topics for Discussion or Writing

1. What health problems can you have if you are overweight?

2. What ways to cook can help you lose weight?

3. What exercises can you do to stay healthy?

## LESSON 4

### Seeing Stars

Lucy is cleaning her house. She knows there is some dust on a high shelf in her living room. She wants to clean it off. Lucy picks up a dust cloth and climbs up on a wobbly, old chair. She reaches up very high. Then the chair tips over, and Lucy falls backwards. She hits her head on the floor. Her husband hears the crash and runs into the room.

Lucy's husband is very upset. Lucy is **conscious,** but she isn't speaking clearly. She says, "I am seeing stars."

Sometimes a head **injury** is very dangerous. Lucy's husband takes her to the hospital. A doctor examines Lucy at the hospital. He asks her many questions. He tests her **balance** and **reflexes.** Lucy has a special brain **x-ray** called a **CAT scan.**

The doctor says Lucy's head injury is a **concussion.** That means there is some injury to her brain. She can take pain **medication.** She also needs to rest at home. "No dusting," says the doctor. "And get a stepladder. No more climbing on wobbly old chairs.

Lucy and her husband leave the hospital. Lucy looks up and says, "I'm seeing stars again."

"Oh, no!" says her husband. "Let's go back inside and tell the doctor!"

"It's OK," says Lucy. "It's nighttime. Those really are stars."

## Answer the questions.

1. What is Lucy doing?

2. Where is there some dust?

3. What does she climb up on?

4. Which way does Lucy fall?

5. What does she hit on the floor?

6. Who hears the crash?

7. Where does her husband take her?

8. What is her special brain x-ray called?

9. What kind of head injury does Lucy have?

10. What does she need to do at home?

# Check the sentence that means the same.

1. Lucy picks up a dust cloth and climbs up on a wobbly, old chair.

____ a. The chair is steady.

_✓_ b. The chair is shaky.

2. Lucy is conscious, but she isn't speaking clearly.

_✓_ a. Lucy is awake, but not talking well.

____ b. Lucy is talking in her sleep.

3. Sometimes a head injury is very dangerous.

____ a. Hitting your head hurts a lot.

_✓_ b. Hitting your head can be a serious problem.

4. A doctor examines Lucy at the hospital.

____ a. He gives her ice and pain medication.

_✓_ b. He asks questions and tests her balance and reflexes.

5. The doctor says Lucy's head injury is a concussion.

____ a. Lucy hurt her back.

_✓_ b. Lucy hurt her brain.

6. "No more climbing on wobbly, old chairs."

_✓_ a. "Only climb on something sturdy."

____ b. "Tell your husband to do the dusting."

## Talking to the Doctor

Practice the dialog with a partner.

**That's a big bump. What happened?**

I fell backward and hit my head on the floor.

**Did you lose consciousness?**

No. But I saw stars.

**Do you know what day it is?**

It's Wednesday. Why do you ask?

**I'm checking your memory and ability to think clearly.**
**We'll need to do some other tests and a CAT scan.**

## Care for Concussion

Read the instructions the doctor gives Lucy's husband. Then answer the questions.

---

### PATIENT INSTRUCTIONS

Wake the patient at least once during the night. Contact the doctor immediately if he or she is difficult to wake or confused. Also, report any vomiting. Give the patient acetaminophen or other aspirin-free medications for headaches. A brain injury is serious. The patient needs rest. He or she needs to wait until the pain or other symptoms are gone before resuming normal activity.

---

1. What does Lucy's husband need to do? _____

2. What does he need to report? _____

3. What can Lucy take for headaches? _____

4. What else does Lucy need? _____

5. When can she resume normal activity? _____

## Sequence the story.

**Put the sentences in the order of the story. Number from 1 to 6.**

_____ Lucy is conscious, but she isn't speaking clearly.

_____ Lucy looks up and says, "I'm seeing stars again."

_____ Lucy has a special brain x-ray called a CAT scan.

_____ Lucy hits her head on the floor.

_____ Lucy's husband takes her to the hospital.

_____ Her husband hears the crash and runs into the room.


## Checklist

**These are some symptoms of a concussion. Put a check next to the symptoms Lucy has.**

_____ seeing stars                    _____ memory loss (amnesia)

_____ headache                        _____ unconsciousness

_____ ringing in the ears             _____ sleepiness

_____ unequal pupil size              _____ nausea

_____ unusual eye movements           _____ vomiting

_____ speaking that is not clear      _____ confusion

_____ dizziness                       _____ sensitivity to light

## What about you?

Check *Yes* or *No*. Then write the questions and ask your partner.

**Yes    No**

____  ____    1. I sometimes climb up on wobbly, old chairs.

   *Do you sometimes climb up on wobbly old chairs?*

____  ____    2. I sometimes take family or friends to the hospital.

   _____

____  ____    3. I think a head injury is very dangerous.

   _____

____  ____    4. I think a concussion is serious.

   _____

____  ____    5. I think it's a good idea to use a sturdy stepladder.

   _____

## Topics for Discussion or Writing

1. What sports or activities can be dangerous for your head?

2. What are some ways you can prevent getting a concussion?

3. Did you ever hit your head? If so, how did it happen? What were your symptoms? Did you go to the hospital?

# LESSON 5

## Walking and Weights

Vita is 71 years old. She is retired and lives in an apartment with her dog, Coco. Vita is not an active person. She pays a neighbor to walk Coco every day. Coco has a lot of **energy,** and Vita is very tired. Coco is always excited to see Vita's neighbor.

One day Vita visits her doctor about some back pain. The doctor asks her about **exercise.**

"Exercise?" asks Vita. "At my age?"

"It's very important at your age," says the doctor. "Exercise helps make your **muscles** stronger. It helps your **bones.** It slows the progress of osteoporosis. That's a disease that makes your bones break easily. You need to think about that." The doctor recommends walking and using **weights.**

The next day Vita starts walking. She takes Coco with her. She walks a quarter mile each day for the first two weeks. After five weeks, Vita can walk one mile. Now she walks at least one mile almost every day. She also uses weights three times a week. Her back feels much better too.

Vita doesn't need her neighbor to walk Coco anymore. She has extra money to spend on good walking shoes and hand weights. Now Coco is excited when Vita gets ready for a walk. And they both have a lot of energy.

## Answer the questions.

1. How old is Vita?    71 yrs

2. Who does she live with?

3. Who does she pay to walk Coco every day?

4. Why does Vita visit the doctor?

5. What does exercise do for muscles and bones?

6. What does the doctor recommend?

7. How far does Vita walk each day for the first two weeks?

8. How far can she walk after five weeks?

9. How often does Vita use weights?

10. What does she have extra money to spend on?

# Check the sentence that means the same.

1. Vita is not an active person.

  ____ a. She exercises a lot.

  ✓ b. She doesn't get a lot of exercise.

2. "It's very important at your age," says the doctor.

  ✓ a. Older people need exercise too.

  ____ b. Older people don't need to exercise.

3. It slows the progress of osteoporosis.

  ✓ a. Exercise helps make your bones stronger.

  ____ b. Exercise helps your bones to break easily.

4. The doctor recommends walking and using weights.

  ____ a. The doctor suggests that Vita join a health club.

  ✓ b. The doctor suggests exercises that Vita can do on her own.

5. Now she walks at least one mile almost every day.

  ✓ a. Vita walks about seven miles a week.

  ____ b. Vita walks about 70 miles a week.

6. Vita doesn't need her neighbor to walk Coco anymore.

  ✓ a. Vita takes Coco with her when she walks.

  ____ b. Vita pays a neighbor to walk Coco.

## Talking to the Doctor

**Practice the dialog with a partner.**

How often do you exercise?

**Exercise? At my age?**

It's very important at your age.

**How can it help?**

It slows the progress of osteoporosis.

**What's that?**

It's a disease that makes your bones break easily.

**I don't want that.**

You need to start walking and using weights.

## Exercise for Seniors

**Read the information the doctor gives Vita. Then answer the questions.**

> Walking is an excellent exercise. Try to walk at least one mile a day. It helps the bones in your legs, hips, and lower spine. It is also inexpensive. You only need a good pair of walking shoes. Lifting weights can build muscles and bones in your arms and upper spine. Both exercises can slow the progress of osteoporosis, a disease that makes your bones break easily.

1. How far does Vita need to walk a day? _____ one mile a day.

2. Which bones does walking help? _____

3. Which muscles and bones can lifting weights build? _____

4. What is osteoporosis? _____

## Write the distance you hear.

1. 1 mile

2. 10 feet

3. 30 miles

4. 1 and half mile

5. _____

6. _____

7. _____

8. _____

9. _____

10. _____

11. _____

12. _____

## Checklist

These are some things some people use for walking. Check the things you think Vita needs. Write other useful items on the lines.

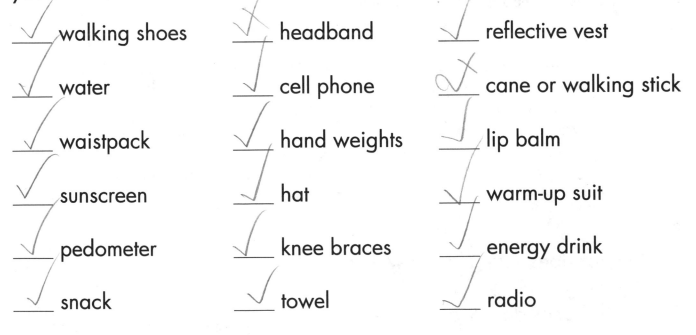

- ✓ walking shoes
- ✓ water
- ✓ waistpack
- ✓ sunscreen
- ✓ pedometer
- ✓ snack

- ✓ headband
- ✓ cell phone
- ✓ hand weights
- ✓ hat
- ✓ knee braces
- ✓ towel

- ✓ reflective vest
- ✓ cane or walking stick
- ✓ lip balm
- ✓ warm-up suit
- ✓ energy drink
- ✓ radio

_____   _____   _____

## What about you?

Check *Yes* or *No*. Then write the questions and ask your partner.

**Yes    No**

____ ____    1. I live in an apartment with a dog.

<u>*Do you live in an apartment with a dog?*</u>

____ ____    2. I think I am an active person.

_____

____ ____    3. I think exercise is important at every age.

_____

____ ____    4. I like walking and using weights.

_____

____ ____    5. I walk at least one mile almost every day.

_____

## Topics for Discussion or Writing

1. What exercises can be good for an older person to do?

2. Where is a good place to walk in your community?

3. What diseases can exercise help prevent?

# LESSON 6

## No Room for Wisdom Teeth

Ling is a 20-year-old college student. Right now she is sitting in the dentist's chair. "How is college?" asks the dentist.

"It's difficult," says Ling. "Studying isn't fun."

The dentist laughs. Then he says, "You have very good teeth. The problem is with your third **molars,** or **wisdom teeth.** You need to have them taken out."

"Why?" asks Ling.

"They are **impacted,**" says the dentist. "That means the teeth are coming in, but there is no room for them. You can get **infections** and other problems. Your wisdom teeth can hurt your other teeth. I can't **extract** them. You need **oral surgery** for that."

Ling's mother takes her to an **oral surgeon,** Dr. Blair. Dr. Blair gives her an **anesthetic.** Then she takes out Ling's four wisdom teeth.

Ling sleeps through the surgery. Later, she wakes up. She has some **bleeding** and **swelling.** She can take **medication** for the pain. She needs **antibiotics** to prevent infection. Ling has instructions about **diet** and caring for her mouth at home. She needs to return to the oral surgeon in one week. Dr. Blair tells her to call if there are any problems.

Ling leaves the office. She turns to her mother. "I love college," she says. "Studying is much more fun than oral surgery."

**Answer the questions.**

1. How old is Ling?

2. What does the dentist say about her wisdom teeth?

3. Why do they need to be taken out?

4. What can Ling's wisdom teeth do to her other teeth?

5. Where does Ling's mother take her?

6. What does the oral surgeon give her?

7. How many wisdom teeth does the oral surgeon take out?

8. What does Ling have when she wakes up?

9. Why does she need antibiotics?

10. When does she need to return to the oral surgeon?

# Which category is it?

| | | | |
|---|---|---|---|
| anesthetic | dentist | orthodontist | periodontist |
| antibiotics | infection | pain | special diet |
| bleeding | oral surgeon | pain medication | swelling |

| Dental Professionals | Problems after Surgery | Things Ling Needs |
|---|---|---|
| 1. _____ | 1. _____ | 1. _____ |
| 2. _____ | 2. _____ | 2. _____ |
| 3. _____ | 3. _____ | 3. _____ |
| 4. _____ | 4. _____ | 4. _____ |

## Matching: Definitions

____ 1. extract       a. the third molars

____ 2. swelling       b. an operation inside the mouth

____ 3. oral surgery       c. when there is no room for a tooth to come in

____ 4. bleeding       d. an area of the body that gets larger

____ 5. wisdom teeth       e. to take out

____ 6. impacted       f. losing blood from the body

## Talking to the Oral Surgeon

Practice the dialog with a partner.

How did the surgery go?

**Fine. I extracted all four wisdom teeth.**

What's in her mouth now?

**That's gauze. Biting down on it helps stop the bleeding.**

How long does she need to do that?

**She can bite on the gauze from time to time for the first 24 hours. She needs to do that until the bleeding stops.**

What can I do if the bleeding doesn't stop?

**Call the office immediately.**

## Swelling after Oral Surgery

Read the information the oral surgeon gives Ling's mother. Then answer the questions.

> Swelling is common for two or three days after you have your wisdom teeth taken out. Use an ice bag for 24 hours. Hold it on the jaw for 30 minutes. Then take it off for 15 minutes. Use pillows to elevate your head while you rest or sleep. A fever or a bad taste in your mouth can be a sign of an infection. Call the office immediately if you have any problems.

1. What is common after you have your wisdom teeth taken out?

_____

2. How long do you use an ice bag? _____

3. What can you use to elevate your head? _____

4. What can be signs of an infection? _____

## Sequence the story.

**Put the sentences in the order of the story. Number from 1 to 6.**

_____ Dr. Blair gives her an anesthetic.

_____ Ling's mother takes her to an oral surgeon.

_____ Ling wakes up. She has some bleeding and swelling.

_____ Ling is sitting in the dentist's chair.

_____ Then she takes out Ling's four wisdom teeth.

_____ The dentist says Ling's teeth are impacted.

## Problem Solving

A dentist tells you that you need to have oral surgery. What can you do? Check the good ideas. Write other good ideas on the lines.

_____ I can ask for a referral to an oral surgeon.

_____ I can get another opinion about my problem.

_____ I can forget about it. Maybe the dentist is wrong.

_____ I can ask a lot of questions about oral surgery.

_____ I can try to extract the teeth myself.

_____ I can tell the dentist that I am afraid of oral surgery.

__✓__ I can _____

__✓__ I can _____

# What about you?

**Check *Yes* or *No*. Then write the questions and ask your partner.**

**Yes    No**

____  ____    1. I have my wisdom teeth.

              *Do you have your wisdom teeth?* _____

____  ____    2. I go to the dentist when I have problems with my teeth.

              _____

____  ____    3. I sometimes go to an oral surgeon.

              _____

____  ____    4. I sometimes have an anesthetic.

              _____

____  ____    5. I follow instructions from a dentist or doctor carefully.

              _____

## Topics for Discussion or Writing

1. For what reasons can you see a dentist?

2. For what reasons can you see an oral surgeon?

3. Why is it important to have someone with you after you have an anesthetic? Who can you bring with you if you have oral surgery?

# LESSON 7

## The Chicken Casserole

Andre and his wife, Marie, are sitting at their dinner table. They are eating chicken casserole. "This is delicious," says Marie. "And there are enough leftovers to eat another day."

Andre jumps up from the table. "Is the casserole still out? We need to put it in the refrigerator right away."

"Don't worry," says Marie. "The food is still warm. I can put it away later. It came out of the oven only 30 minutes ago."

"We need to put it away now," says Andre. "**Bacteria** can grow quickly. **Food poisoning** is a terrible thing. We don't want to get sick." Andre finds a shallow container and puts the leftover casserole inside. He covers it with a lid that fits tightly. He also writes the date on the container.

Andre puts the casserole in the refrigerator. Then he checks that the temperature inside the refrigerator is 40 degrees Fahrenheit.

Four days later, Andre is very hungry. He remembers the delicious chicken casserole. He looks in the refrigerator, but he doesn't see it. "Where is the leftover chicken casserole, Marie?" asks Andre.

"Sorry," says Marie. "Some foods can go bad after two or three days in the refrigerator. I know you don't want to get sick. I threw it away yesterday."

## Answer the questions.

1. What are Andre and his wife eating?

2. Where does Andre want to put the casserole right away?

3. How long ago did it come out of the oven?

4. What can grow quickly?

5. What kind of a container does Andre put the casserole inside?

6. What does he cover it with?

7. What does he write on the container?

8. What is the temperature inside of the refrigerator when Andre checks?

9. How many days later does Andre remember the casserole?

10. Where is the casserole?

## Check the sentence that means the same.

1. We need to put it in the refrigerator right away.

____ a. The casserole needs to go in the refrigerator in 30 minutes.

____ b. The casserole needs to go in the refrigerator right now.

2. Bacteria can grow quickly.

____ a. Germs can multiply fast.

____ b. All casseroles have germs.

3. We don't want to get sick.

____ a. We don't want food poisoning.

____ b. We don't want leftover food.

4. He also writes a date on the container.

____ a. Andre writes the time on the outside.

____ b. Andre writes the month and day on the outside.

5. Some foods go bad after two or three days in the refrigerator.

____ a. Some foods get more delicious after a few days.

____ b. Some foods grow bacteria after a few days.

6. I threw it away yesterday.

____ a. I put the leftover casserole in the garbage.

____ b. I ate the leftover casserole.

## Asking about Food Poisoning

**Practice the dialog with a partner.**

I feel terrible. I think I have food poisoning.

**What are your symptoms?**

I am vomiting and have diarrhea.

**You need to drink a lot of liquid and rest.**

Is there any medication I can take?

**No. And don't take medications that stop diarrhea.**

Why not?

**The bacteria need to leave your system.**

## Food Poisoning Prevention

**Read about the prevention of food poisoning. Then answer the questions.**

> Throw away food that is not refrigerated within two hours. The temperature in your refrigerator should be no higher than 40 degrees Fahrenheit. Never taste food that you don't know about. It may not be safe even if it looks and smells good. Food that is left out too long can have bacteria. Keep leftovers in the refrigerator no longer than four days.

1. What food should you throw away? _____

2. What should the temperature in your refrigerator be? _____

3. Is food always safe if it looks and smells good? _____

4. What can food that is left out too long have? _____

5. How long can you keep leftovers in the refrigerator? _____

# Sequence the pictures.

**Listen. Then number the pictures in the correct order.**

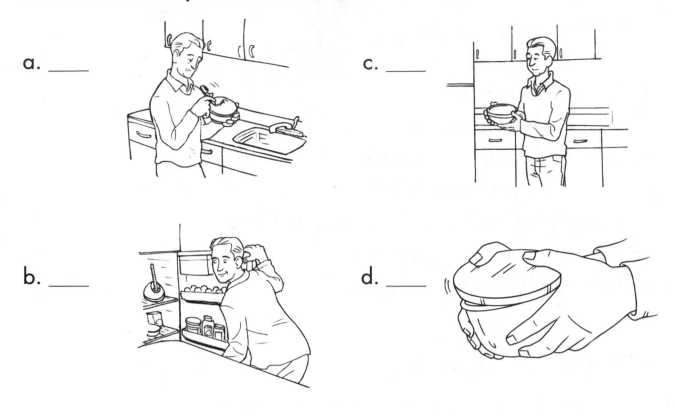

a. ____

c. ____

b. ____

d. ____

# Problem Solving

You are hungry. You aren't sure about something in the refrigerator. What can you do? Check the good ideas. Write other good ideas on the lines.

____ I can eat it later in the week.          ____ I can taste a little bit.

____ I can smell it and check if it's OK.     ____ I can throw it away.

____ I can eat it all. I don't like to waste food.

____ I can ask when it went into the refrigerator.

✔ I can _____

✔ I can _____

## What about you?

Check *Yes* or *No*. Then write the questions and ask your partner.

**Yes    No**

____  ____    1. I eat a lot of leftovers.

*Do you eat a lot of leftovers?* _____

____  ____    2. I put leftover food in the refrigerator right away.

_____

____  ____    3. I put food into the refrigerator within two hours.

_____

____  ____    4. I check the temperature inside my refrigerator.

_____

____  ____    5. I throw away leftover food in the refrigerator after two or three days.

_____

## Topics for Discussion or Writing

1. What are some ways to prevent food poisoning?

2. How do you know that a food is not safe to eat? What things can you look for before throwing it away?

## LESSON 8

### Coughing and Sneezing

Alek is a taxi driver. He works ten-hour shifts, six days a week. Alek needs to work hard to support his family. Right now Alek isn't feeling well. He has a bad **cold,** and he's **coughing** and **sneezing** a lot. It's difficult to rest because he is working all the time.

Alek can see that his passengers are unhappy. When he is coughing and sneezing, they turn their heads away from him. They don't want to catch his **virus.** This morning an angry woman got out of his taxi and said, "Thanks for spreading your **germs.** No tip for you!"

Alek stops at a **pharmacy** and looks for some medicine. He doesn't want anyone to catch his cold. He picks up one that says it's for coughs and colds. He knows it can't **cure** a virus, but maybe it can help him stop coughing and sneezing.

Alek reads the label carefully. It says, "This **medication** may cause **dizziness** or **drowsiness.** Be careful when driving or operating machinery." He picks up a few other cold medicines. They have the same **warning.**

Alek decides he can't take these medicines and drive a taxi. It's too dangerous. He needs to take some time off to get better. Alek needs the money, but he also needs happy passengers who give tips.

## Answer the questions.

1. What is Alek's occupation?

2. When does he work?

3. Why does Alek need to work hard?

4. How is Alek feeling right now?

5. What do his passengers do when he's coughing and sneezing?

6. What did an angry woman say this morning?

7. What does Alek look for at the pharmacy?

8. What does he read carefully?

9. What does the label say?

10. What does Alek decide to do?

## Check the sentence that means the same.

1. It's difficult to rest because he is working all the time.

_____ a. Alek works very little and has a lot of time to rest.

_____ b. Alek works a lot and doesn't have time to rest.

2. Alek stops at a pharmacy.

_____ a. He wants to go to a drugstore when he stops working.

_____ b. He goes into a drugstore.

3. This medication may cause dizziness or drowsiness.

_____ a. This medicine can make you feel unsteady or sleepy.

_____ b. This medicine can make you feel very sick.

4. Be careful when driving or operating machinery.

_____ a. It's a good idea to take this medicine and drive.

_____ b. It's not a good idea to take this medicine and drive.

5. Alek decides he can't take these medicines and drive a taxi.

_____ a. Alek will stop driving so that he can take the medicine.

_____ b. Alek won't take the medicine, and he won't drive.

6. He needs to take some time off to get better.

_____ a. Alek has to rest at home to feel better.

_____ b. Alek has to rest in his taxi.

## Talking to the Pharmacist

Practice the dialog with a partner.

What can you recommend for coughing and sneezing?

**This cold medicine can help you.**

I drive a lot. Is that OK?

**No. This medicine can make you feel sleepy.**

Is there anything else I can take?

**Here is something that is non-drowsy. It won't make you feel sleepy.**

## Cold Medicine

Read some information on this cold medicine label. Then answer the questions.

> ***Cold-Away*** provides temporary relief of these major symptoms: fever, headache, body aches and pains, runny nose, nasal congestion, sneezing, coughing, sore throat. When using this product, do not use more than directed. You may feel dizziness or drowsiness. Avoid alcoholic drinks. Be careful when driving a motor vehicle or operating machinery.

1. What is the name of the cold medicine? _____

2. Which major symptoms does Alek have? _____

3. How may you feel when you take this medicine? _____

4. What kind of drinks do you need to avoid? _____

5. When do you need to be careful? _____

6. Is this a good medicine for Alek to take? Why or why not? _____

_____

## Sequence the story.

**Put the sentences in the order of the story. Number from 1 to 6.**

_____ Alek stops at a pharmacy.

_____ Alek is coughing and sneezing.

_____ He see that this medication may cause drowsiness.

_____ Alek needs some time off to get better.

_____ He reads the label on the cold medicine carefully.

_____ His passengers turn their heads away from him.

## Problem Solving

You have a bad cold. It's difficult to rest because you're working. What can you do? Check the good ideas. Write other good ideas on the lines.

_____ I can take some time off.                _____ I can eat chicken soup.

_____ I can take non-drowsy cold medicine.     _____ I can rest at work.

_____ I can cough and sneeze at other people.

_____ I can take cold medicine that causes drowsiness.

_____ I can cover my nose and mouth to not spread germs.

✓ I can _____

✓ I can _____

## What about you?

Check *Yes* or *No*. Then write the questions and ask your partner.

**Yes    No**

\_\_\_\_  \_\_\_\_  1. I work hard to support my family.

<u>Do you work hard</u> to support your family?

\_\_\_\_  \_\_\_\_  2. I turn my head away when people cough and sneeze.

_____

\_\_\_\_  \_\_\_\_  3. I take cold medicine when I am not feeling well.

_____

\_\_\_\_  \_\_\_\_  4. I read medicine labels carefully.

_____

\_\_\_\_  \_\_\_\_  5. I take time off to get better when I am sick.

_____

## Topics for Discussion or Writing

1. What symptoms do you have when you're not feeling well? What do you do for them?

2. How do you not spread germs when you have a cold?

3. When is it dangerous to take medicine that causes drowsiness? Why?

## LESSON 9

### A Busy Nurse-Practitioner

Mara Flynn is a **nurse-practitioner.** She works in a busy doctor's office. Every day Mara talks to many **patients** on the telephone. Today Mara is talking to Mr. Avila. He has a cold. But his **symptoms** are not serious. "Please call the **pharmacy,**" he says. "I need **antibiotics.**"

"It doesn't sound like a **bacterial infection,**" says Mara. "You have a **virus.** Antibiotics can't help you."

Mr. Avila is disappointed. He thinks he can feel better faster with antibiotics. But Mara tells him this is not true. She says, "Never take antibiotics when you don't need them. Taking antibiotics too much can make bacteria **antibiotic-resistant.** Then antibiotics don't work when you really need them."

Mara receives many more phone calls that day. Mrs. Tweed has a **cough.** Mr. Webb has the **flu.** Miss Lee has a stomachache. They all want antibiotics. Again, Mara says, "Antibiotics can't help you."

Mara comes home from work that evening. Her husband is at home. He is taking care of their four-year-old daughter, Rose. "She still has a **fever,**" says her husband.

"My ear hurts a lot!" says Rose. Mara looks in Rose's ear with an **otoscope.**

"Oh, dear, Rose," says Mara. This looks like a bacterial infection. You need antibiotics."

## Answer the questions.

1. What is Mara Flynn's job?

2. Where does she work?

3. What does Mr. Avila say he needs?

4. What can happen to bacteria when you take antibiotics too much?

5. What do Mrs. Tweed, Mr. Webb, and Miss Lee want?

6. What does Mara say to them?

7. What's the matter with Mara's four-year-old daughter?

8. What does Mara use to look in Rose's ear?

9. What does Mara see in Rose's ear?

10. What does Rose need?

## Check the sentence that means the same.

1. He has a cold. But his symptoms are not serious.

    _____ a. He has a runny nose and a cough. But he isn't very sick.

    _____ b. He has a high fever and a terrible sore throat.

2. You have a virus. Antibiotics can't help you.

    _____ a. Antibiotics can make you feel better faster.

    _____ b. Antibiotics don't cure a virus.

3. Taking antibiotics too much can make bacteria antibiotic-resistant.

    _____ a. There are many different antibiotics that kill bacteria.

    _____ b. Antibiotics stop working if people take them when they are
            not needed.

4. Mrs. Tweed has a cough. Mr. Webb has the flu. Miss Lee has a
   stomachache.

    _____ a. They all have infections from viruses.

    _____ b. They all have infections from bacteria.

5. She still has a fever.

    _____ a. Her body temperature is still high.

    _____ b. She is feeling much better.

6. This looks like a bacterial infection. You need antibiotics.

    _____ a. Antibiotics can help you.

    _____ b. Antibiotics can't help you.

## Talking to a Nurse-Practitioner

**Practice the dialog with a partner.**

I need antibiotics. Can you call the pharmacy for me?

**What are your symptoms?**

I have a runny nose and a cough.

**You have a virus. Antibiotics can't help you.**

What can I do?

**Drink plenty of fluids and rest.**

## Using Antibiotics

**Read some information about antibiotics. Then answer the questions.**

Most infections come from bacteria or viruses. Antibiotics can help bacterial infections. They do not work if you have a virus. Taking antibiotics when you don't need them can make bacteria antibiotic-resistant. This can lead to more serious health problems.
**Bacterial infections:** strep throat, some ear infections, urinary tract infections, some sinus infections, many wound and skin infections
**Viral infections:** colds, flu, most sore throats, most coughs

1. What can antibiotics help? _____

2. What happens if you take antibiotics when you don't need them?

_____

3. Should you take antibiotics for strep throat and skin infections? _____

4. Should you take antibiotics for colds and flu? _____

## Sequence the pictures.

**Listen. Then number the pictures in the correct order.**

a. ____

c. ____

b. ____

d. ____

## Checklist

You have a cold or flu virus. You want to feel better faster. Check the things that can help you. Write other useful items on the lines.

____ antibiotics

____ fluids

____ antihistamine

____ soup

____ pain medicine

____ nasal spray

____ tea with honey

____ vitamin C

____ decongestant

____ aspirin

____ lozenges

____ herbal remedy

____ antibiotic injections

____ orange juice

____ flu shot

____ cough syrup

____ antiseptic mouthwash

____ zinc

_____

_____

_____

## What about you?

Check *Yes* or *No*. Then write the questions and ask your partner.

**Yes    No**

____  ____    1. I sometimes talk to a nurse-practitioner on the telephone.

<u>Do you sometimes talk to a nurse-practitioner on the</u>

<u>telephone?</u>

____  ____    2. I think antibiotics can always make me feel better faster.

_____

____  ____    3. I take antibiotics for infections from viruses.

_____

____  ____    4. I take antibiotics for infections from bacteria.

_____

____  ____    5. I think antibiotics can sometimes help an ear infection.

_____

## Topics for Discussion or Writing

1. Do you take antibiotics? If so, when? How long do you take them?

2. What are good things to ask a nurse-practitioner on the telephone?

3. When is it a good idea to go to the doctor's office?

# LESSON 10

## Tonsils Out

Nika is seven years old. She has very large **tonsils.** She is sick a lot. Nika gets **throat infections** called **tonsillitis. Swallowing** is difficult. It hurts to eat and drink. It's also difficult for Nika to breathe. She **snores** loudly at night when she sleeps. The noise keeps her mother and father awake in the next room. They worry that her breathing is loud and irregular. No one in the family sleeps well. In the morning, Nika and her parents are exhausted.

Nika's parents take her to an ear, nose, and throat doctor. Nika's parents talk about Nika's health history. The doctor examines her throat for a long time. She recommends that Nika have an **operation** to take out her tonsils. The operation is called a **tonsillectomy.**

Soon Nika goes to the hospital. Her operation takes only about 20 minutes. In a few hours, she goes home. She eats food that feels soft on her throat. She has ice pops, gelatin, ice cream, and soup. After two weeks, Nika feels much better.

Nika is fine now. She doesn't have any throat infections. Her breathing is very quiet at night when she sleeps. Now Nika's father is the only person snoring loudly. Nika's mother covers her ears. Maybe she can take him to the ear, nose, and throat doctor too.

## Answer the questions.

1. How old is Nika?

2. What are her throat infections called?

3. What does she do at night when she sleeps?

4. How do Nika and her parents feel in the morning?

5. Where do Nika's parents bring her?

6. What does the doctor recommend?

7. What is the operation called?

8. How long does the operation take?

9. What can Nika eat when she goes home?

10. Who is the only person snoring loudly now?

## Which category is it?

| breathing | eating | ice pops | soup |
| drinking | gelatin | neck | swallowing |
| ears | ice cream | nose | throat |

| Parts of the Body | Soft Foods | Activities Affected by Tonsillitis |
|---|---|---|
| 1. _____ | 1. _____ | 1. _____ |
| 2. _____ | 2. _____ | 2. _____ |
| 3. _____ | 3. _____ | 3. _____ |
| 4. _____ | 4. _____ | 4. _____ |

## Matching: Definitions

____ 1. exhausted

____ 2. throat

____ 3. tonsillitis

____ 4. snore

____ 5. tonsillectomy

____ 6. swallowing

a. a throat infection

b. moving liquid or solids from the mouth down the throat

c. to breathe loudly while sleeping

d. the part of the body at the back of the mouth

e. an operation to take out the tonsils

f. very tired

## Talking to the Ear, Nose, and Throat Doctor

**Practice the dialog with a partner.**

My daughter snores very loudly.

**Is her breathing irregular?**

Yes, it is. It starts and stops. She's exhausted in the morning.

**Tell me about her health history.**

She is sick a lot. She has tonsillitis several times a year.

**A tonsillectomy can probably help her.**

## Preparing for a Tonsillectomy

**Read this information the doctor gives Nika's parents. Then answer the questions.**

> Do not give your child anything to eat or drink the night before the surgery. Your child will have anesthesia and feel no pain during the operation. A tonsillectomy takes only about 20 minutes. A sore throat is normal after the operation. It's important to give your child fluids right away. Most children go home on the day of the operation. It takes about two weeks to recover completely.

1. What must you not give your child the night before the surgery?

   _____

2. How long does a tonsillectomy take? _____

3. After the surgery, what do you need to give your child right away?

   _____

4. When do most children go home? _____

5. How long does it take to recover completely? _____

## Sequence the story.

**Put the sentences in the order of the story. Number from 1 to 6.**

_____ Nika's parents take her to an ear, nose, and throat doctor.

_____ Nika goes to the hospital. Her operation takes only about 20 minutes.

_____ She recommends that Nika have an operation to take out her tonsils.

_____ After two weeks, Nika feels much better.

_____ Nika snores loudly at night when she sleeps.

_____ The doctor examines her throat for a long time.

## Checklist

Your child is home after a tonsillectomy. Check the food and drinks that are good for her to eat while she recovers. Write other good things on the lines.

| | | |
|---|---|---|
| _____ ice pops | _____ pasta | _____ popcorn |
| _____ potato chips | _____ pudding | _____ cooked fruit |
| _____ apple juice | _____ ice chips | _____ toast |
| _____ scrambled eggs | _____ yogurt | _____ ice cream |
| _____ gelatin | _____ cooked cereal | _____ soup |
| _____ orange juice | _____ raw vegetables | _____ mashed potatoes |

_____  _____  _____

# What about you?

Check *Yes* or *No*. Then write the questions and ask your partner.

**Yes    No**

____  ____    1. I still have my tonsils.

__*Do you still have your tonsils?*_____

____  ____    2. I get tonsillitis a lot.

_____

____  ____    3. I snore loudly at night when I sleep.

_____

____  ____    4. I sleep well at night.

_____

____  ____    5. I sometimes see a doctor for problems with my ears, nose, or throat.

_____

## Topics for Discussion or Writing

1. How can you help someone who snores loudly?

2. Do you have your tonsils out? What happened at your operation?

3. What other things can you do for tonsillitis?

## LESSON 11

### Missing a Vaccine

Liem Nguyen and his son, Tai, are standing in the office of Big Rock Middle School. Liem is registering Tai for the sixth grade. Tai doesn't want to start school on Monday. Tai likes summer. He doesn't want to have homework again. Liem fills out many forms. The **school nurse** is also there. She is checking **immunization records.** Liem gives her a yellow card. The card shows his son's **immunizations.** The nurse says, "Your son is missing his third **dose** of the **hepatitis B vaccine.**"

"Does he need it?" asks Liem.

"Yes," says the nurse. "We can't register him for school without it."

"What is hepatitis B?" asks Liem.

"Hepatitis B is a serious disease. It is caused by a **virus** that attacks the **liver.** Your son needs protection from it."

Then the school nurse gives Liem some information from the Public Health Department. They give immunizations at their **clinic** every Friday.

On Friday, Liem takes Tai to the clinic. Tai gets his third dose of the hepatitis B vaccine. Now Tai has all of the immunizations he needs for school. He can start with the other children on Monday.

"You are all ready for school," says Liem. "Are you excited?"

"Let me look at my yellow card again," says Tai. "Maybe I am missing something else."

## Answer the questions.

1. Where are Liem and Tai standing?

2. For what grade is Liem registering Tai?

3. What does Liem fill out?

4. Who is checking immunization records?

5. What is Tai missing?

6. What is hepatitis B?

7. What does the school nurse give Liem?

8. When does the Public Health Department give immunizations?

9. What does Tai get at the clinic?

10. When can Tai start school?

## Which category is it?

| | | | |
|---|---|---|---|
| birth certificate | hepatitis B | measles | proof of home address |
| community clinic | hospital | mobile clinic | school records |
| doctor's office | immunization record | polio | tuberculosis |

**Things Necessary for School**

1. _____

2. _____

3. _____

4. _____

**Places to Get Immunizations**

1. _____

2. _____

3. _____

4. _____

**Serious Diseases**

1. _____

2. _____

3. _____

4. _____

## Matching: Definitions

____ 1. hepatitis B      a. the document showing dates of vaccines

____ 2. clinic      b. a disease caused by a virus that attacks the liver

____ 3. register      c. a place to get medical treatment

____ 4. liver      d. to sign up for classes or school

____ 5. dose      e. a measured quantity

____ 6. immunization record      f. an organ in the body that cleans the blood

## Talking to the School Nurse

**Practice the dialog with a partner.**

Your son is missing his third dose of the hepatitis B vaccine.

**Does he need it?**

Yes. We can't register him for school without it.

**What is hepatitis B?**

Hepatitis B is a disease caused by a virus that attacks the liver.

**Where can he get the vaccine?**

The Public Health Department gives immunizations every Friday.

## Immunization Information

**Read the information the school nurse gives Liem. Then answer the questions.**

> The North City Public Health Clinic gives immunizations every Friday. The clinic offers vaccines to protect against polio, measles, mumps, rubella, varicella (chickenpox), hepatitis A, hepatitis B, and others. The cost is $10. Immunizations for children under 2 years of age are free. Clinic hours are 8:00 to 11:00 AM and 1:00 to 4:00 PM.

1. When does the North City Public Health Clinic give immunizations?

   _____

2. Can Tai get his hepatitis B vaccine there? _____

3. How much does Liem need to pay for the vaccine? _____

4. What are the clinic hours? _____

## Sequence the pictures.

Listen. Then number the pictures in the correct order.

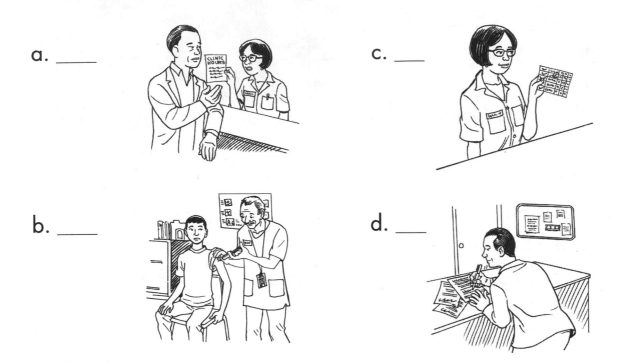

a. ____

c. ____

b. ____

d. ____

## Problem Solving

Your child is missing a vaccine that is necessary for school. What can you do? Check the good ideas. Write other good ideas on the lines.

____ I can get the vaccine at my doctor's office.

____ I can ask the school nurse if I can get the vaccine later.

____ I can change his immunization record.

____ I can look for a clinic that offers the vaccine.

____ I can keep him home until he gets the vaccine.

✓ I can _____

✓ I can _____

## What about you?

Check *Yes* or *No*. Then write the questions and ask your partner.

**Yes    No**

____  ____    1. I have an immunization record for my child.

*Do you have an immunization record for your child?*

____  ____    2. I think hepatitis B is a serious disease.

_____

____  ____    3. I know the location of a public health clinic in my area.

_____

____  ____    4. I think it's important for people to have immunizations.

_____

____  ____    5. I think it's good to check immunization records for school.

_____

## Topics for Discussion or Writing

1. What are some forms you fill out when you register for school?

2. What immunizations do you need to register for school?

3. Where are some places in your community that offer immunizations?

## LESSON 12

### Type 2 Diabetes

Mateo is 12 years old and **overweight.** He eats too many high-**calorie** foods. He drinks a lot of sugary sodas. Lately Mateo feels **thirsty** all the time. He **urinates** often. He doesn't have a lot of **energy.** Mateo's mother is concerned. She takes him to the doctor. The doctor orders several **lab tests** for Mateo.

In a few days, Mateo and his mother go back to the office. The doctor says, "Mateo, you have **type 2 diabetes.** It's a disease that affects how your body uses **glucose.** Glucose is a sugar that your body needs. When you have type 2 diabetes, your blood glucose level is too high. You can get very sick."

Mateo and his mother look worried. Then the doctor says, "Don't worry. Type 2 diabetes is serious, but you can live a long and healthy life."

The doctor gives Mateo and his mother a lot of information. Mateo needs to learn about checking his blood glucose levels. He gets information about **exercise, medication,** and **diet.** Now Mateo needs to avoid high-calorie foods and sodas.

Mateo and his mother leave the office. "There is a vending machine," says Mateo. "May I please have a soda?"

"Sorry, Mateo," says his mother. "Let's listen to the doctor. There is a water fountain outside."

## Answer the questions.

1. How old is Mateo?

2. What does he eat and drink?

3. Why is Mateo's mother concerned?

4. What does the doctor order for Mateo?

5. What does Mateo have?

6. What is too high when a person has type 2 diabetes?

7. What does Mateo need to learn about checking?

8. What does he get information about?

9. What does he need to avoid?

10. What does Mateo want after they leave the office?

## Check the sentence that means the same.

1. Mateo is 12 years old and overweight.

_____ a. He weighs too little for a child of his age.

_____ b. He weighs too much for a child of his age.

2. Lately Mateo feels thirsty all the time.

_____ a. He wants something to drink frequently.

_____ b. He never wants to drink anything.

3. Mateo's mother is concerned.

_____ a. She is worried about him.

_____ b. She knows he is OK.

4. The doctor orders several lab tests for Mateo.

_____ a. Mateo needs to have samples of his blood analyzed.

_____ b. Mateo needs to have his diet analyzed.

5. You have type 2 diabetes.

_____ a. Don't be concerned. You don't have a serious problem.

_____ b. Your blood glucose level is too high. You can get very sick.

6. Now Mateo needs to avoid high-calorie foods and sodas.

_____ a. He can sometimes have unhealthy foods.

_____ b. He needs to stop eating unhealthy foods.

## Talking to the Doctor

**Practice the dialog with a partner.**

How can my son control his type 2 diabetes?

**First he needs to lose weight. It can help lower his blood glucose level.**

What can he eat?

**He needs fruits, vegetables, and whole grains.**

What can't he eat?

**He needs to avoid sugary sodas and processed foods. You can talk to a dietician about his meal plan.**

## Diabetes Diet

**Read the information the doctor gives Mateo and his mother. Then answer the questions.**

> Your diet can help you control your blood glucose levels. Eat fruits, vegetables, and whole grains. The body breaks them down slowly. Then there is a slower release of glucose into the blood stream. Stay away from processed foods like white bread or white rice. The body breaks them down quickly. That leads to a fast rise in blood glucose level. Also, make sure that your portion sizes are not too big. Drink water when you are thirsty. Sugary sodas can add several hundred calories a day to your diet.

1. What can your diet help you control? _____

2. What is good for you to eat? Why? _____

3. What do you need to stay away from? Why? _____

4. What is good to drink when you are thirsty? _____

# Sequence the pictures.

**Listen. Then number the pictures in the correct order.**

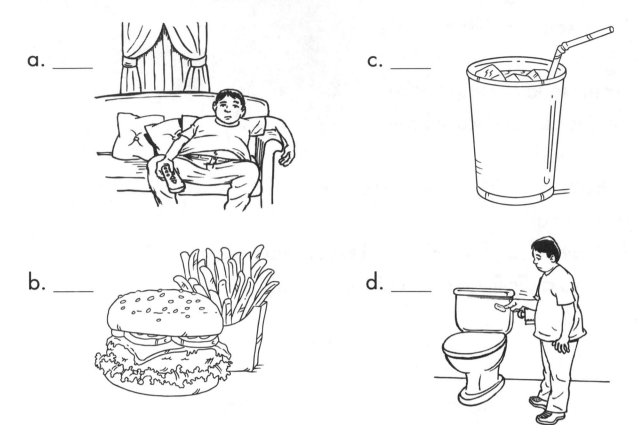

a. _____

c. _____

b. _____

d. _____

# Checklist

Your child has type 2 diabetes. Check the food and drinks that can help him control it. Write other good things on the lines.

_____ strawberries _____ whole wheat pasta _____ lettuce

_____ carrots _____ French fries _____ brown rice

_____ whole grain cereal _____ sugary sodas _____ water

_____ donuts _____ whole wheat bread _____ tomatoes

_____ broccoli _____ white rice _____ candy

_____ white bread _____ oranges _____ sugary cereal

_____ _____ _____

## What about you?

Check *Yes* or *No*. Then write the questions and ask your partner.

**Yes    No**

\_\_\_\_  \_\_\_\_    1. I eat too many high-calorie foods.

*Do you eat too many high-calorie foods?*

\_\_\_\_  \_\_\_\_    2. I drink a lot of sugary sodas.

\_\_\_\_  \_\_\_\_    3. I have a lot of energy.

\_\_\_\_  \_\_\_\_    4. I sometimes have lab tests.

\_\_\_\_  \_\_\_\_    5. I know someone who has type 2 diabetes.

## Topics for Discussion or Writing

1. What kinds of high-calorie foods do children sometimes like to eat?

2. Type 2 diabetes is increasing among children and teenagers. Why do you think it is on the rise?

3. Do you drink sodas? If so, how often do you drink them? What do you usually drink when you are thirsty?

## LESSON 13

### Protect Your Skin from the Sun

Zack lives in Florida. He loves to go to the beach and sit in the sun for hours. Zack doesn't wear a hat or **sunscreen.** He likes getting a tan. He thinks he looks more handsome.

One morning Zack is shaving. He notices a **bump** near his nose. Zack looks at this bump every day. It doesn't go away. He asks his doctor about it. Then his doctor refers him to a doctor for the skin. The doctor is called a **dermatologist.**

The dermatologist does a **biopsy.** He takes a piece of the bump on Zack's face. Then he checks it under a **microscope** for **cancer** cells. Zack's bump is a **basal cell carcinoma.** It's the most common skin cancer. The doctor tells Zack that he needs to remove the bump. Then he cuts it out in the office.

After Zack's surgery, the dermatologist gives him some advice. "You need to protect your skin from the sun!" he says. "Avoid the sun between 10 A.M. and 4 P.M. Wear a long-sleeved shirt and hat when you are outdoors. Always use sunscreen. Check your skin every month for signs of skin cancer. It's important to **treat** skin cancer early."

Now Zack follows the doctor's advice when he goes outside. And when he sees someone getting a tan, Zack says, "Put on a shirt and hat! Use sunscreen! You need to protect your skin from the sun!"

## Answer the questions.

1. Where does Zack live?

2. What does he love to do?

3. What doesn't he wear?

4. What does he notice near his nose?

5. Who does his doctor refer him to?

6. What does the dermatologist do?

7. What is Zack's bump?

8. Where does the dermatologist cut out the bump?

9. What advice does the dermatologist give?

10. How often does Zack need to check his skin?

**Check the sentence that means the same.**

1. He likes getting a tan.

    ____ a. He likes his skin to be lighter.

    ____ b. He likes his skin to be darker.

2. He notices a bump near his nose.

    ____ a. He sees a raised area on his face.

    ____ b. He sees a hole in his face.

3. Then his doctor refers him to a doctor for the skin.

    ____ a. The doctor sends him to a cardiologist.

    ____ b. The doctor sends him to a dermatologist.

4. Then he does a biopsy.

    ____ a. He cuts the whole bump out in the office.

    ____ b. He checks a piece of the bump under a microscope for cancer cells.

5. Zack's bump is a basal cell carcinoma.

    ____ a. It's the most common skin cancer.

    ____ b. It's a very unusual skin cancer.

6. Wear a long-sleeved shirt and hat when you are outdoors.

    ____ a. Cover your body in the sun.

    ____ b. Uncover your body so that you can get a tan.

## Talking to the Dermatologist

Practice the dialog with a partner.

I am concerned about this bump on my face.

**How long have you had it?**

I've had it for about two months.

**Has it changed in size and appearance?**

No. It's just a pink, shiny bump that doesn't go away.

**It looks like a skin cancer.**

Oh, no! Is this something I need to worry about?

**Don't worry. Most skin cancers are curable with early treatment.**

## Sun Protection Advice

Read the information the dermatologist gives Zack. Then answer the questions.

> - Avoid the sun between 10 A.M. and 4 P.M.
> - Wear a long-sleeved shirt, a wide-brimmed hat, and UV-blocking sunglasses when you are outdoors.
> - Use sunscreen with a sun protection factor (SPF) of 15 or higher.
> - Check your skin every month for signs of skin cancer.
> - Treat skin cancer as early as possible.

1. At what times should you avoid the sun? _____

2. What should you wear outdoors? _____

3. Which sunscreen SPF should you use? _____

4. How often should you check your skin for skin cancer? _____

5. When should you treat skin cancer? _____

## Sequence the story.

**Put the sentences in the order of the story. Number from 1 to 6.**

_____ The dermatologist does a biopsy.

_____ The dermatologist cuts it out in the office.

_____ His doctor refers him to a doctor for the skin, called a dermatologist.

_____ One morning Zack is shaving. He notices a bump near his nose.

_____ After Zack's surgery, the dermatologist gives him some advice.

_____ Zack learns his bump is a basal cell carcinoma.

## Checklist

You need to be outdoors for a long time. Check the things that can help you protect your skin from the sun. Write other good things on the lines.

_____ sunscreen SPF 15 or higher          _____ umbrella

_____ long-sleeved shirt          _____ sun tan oil SPF 6

_____ UV-blocking sunglasses          _____ white, short-sleeved T-shirt

_____ bathing suit          _____ wide-brimmed hat

_____ backwards baseball cap          _____ non-UV-blocking sunglasses

_____ long pants          _____ tent for shade

_____          _____

## What about you?

Check *Yes* or *No*. Then write the questions and ask your partner.

**Yes    No**

____  ____    1. I avoid the sun between 10 A.M. and 4 P.M.

<u>**Do you avoid the sun between 10 AM and 4 PM?**</u>

____  ____    2. I always wear sunscreen with an SPF of 15 or higher.

_____

____  ____    3. I wear a wide-brimmed hat, a long-sleeved shirt, and UV-blocking sunglasses outdoors.

_____

____  ____    4. I check my skin every month for signs of skin cancer.

_____

## Topics for Discussion or Writing

1. Do you do activities outdoors? If so, what activities do you do? How do you protect your skin from the sun?

2. Do you check for signs of skin cancer? If so, what do you check for?

3. Does your doctor ever refer you to another doctor? If so, what is that doctor called? What names of other medical specialists do you know?

# LESSON 14

## The Bee Sting

Today Elena is wearing a bright, flowery dress and a fragrant perfume. Right now she is having lunch in a little garden outside her office. Elena is eating a peanut butter and jelly sandwich and drinking lemonade. Soon a bee is buzzing around her. Elena swats it away. But the bee gets annoyed. It stings Elena's arm.

"Ouch," says Elena. She brushes off the **stinger** with her **fingernail.** Elena goes into the restroom to wash the bee sting with soap and water. Then Elena gets the rest of her lunch and goes back to her desk.

Soon Elena starts **coughing.** Then she begins to **sneeze** and **itch.** She also gets a **rash.** "I got stung by a bee," she says to her co-worker, Derek. "I'm having an **allergic reaction.**"

Derek takes her to the hospital **emergency room.** Elena gets an **injection** and other **medication.** Later she feels better. "You were right to come to the emergency room," says the doctor. "An allergic reaction is serious. More people **die** from bee stings than snake bites."

Now Elena carries medication in case a bee stings her again. She only wears light-colored clothing. She doesn't wear any perfume.

"Would you like to join me for lunch in the garden?" asks another co-worker.

"No thanks," says Elena. "I'm eating at my desk."

## Answer the questions.

1. What is Elena wearing?

2. Where is she eating lunch?

3. What is she eating?

4. Where does the bee sting Elena?

5. What does she do in the restroom?

6. What happens at her desk?

7. Where does her co-worker take her?

8. What does she get in the emergency room?

9. What does Elena carry now?

10. What does she wear now?

## Which category is it?

| | | | |
|---|---|---|---|
| bright colors | garden | pain reliever | sneeze |
| cough | ice pack | perfume | soap |
| food | itch | rash | water |

| Things that Attract Bees | Signs of Allergic Reaction | Things to Help a Bee Sting |
|---|---|---|
| 1. _____ | 1. _____ | 1. _____ |
| 2. _____ | 2. _____ | 2. _____ |
| 3. _____ | 3. _____ | 3. _____ |
| 4. _____ | 4. _____ | 4. _____ |

## Matching: Opposites

____ 1. fragrant        a. unimportant

____ 2. die        b. worse

____ 3. bright        c. live

____ 4. annoyed        d. unscented

____ 5. better        e. inside

____ 6. outside        f. light-colored

____ 7. serious        g. pleased

## Talking to the Emergency Room Doctor

Practice the dialog with a partner.

What did you give me?

**We gave you an injection to help you breathe.**

What are you giving me now?

**It's an antihistamine for the rash.**

Can this happen again if another bee stings me?

**Yes. You will always need to carry medication with you.**

An allergic reaction is really scary.


## Treating a Bee Sting

Read the information about treating a bee sting. Then answer the questions.

> - Gently scrape or brush off the stinger. Use gauze or a straight-edged object like a credit card, the back of a knife, or a long fingernail. Never squeeze the stinger or use tweezers. You can cause more venom to go into the skin.
> - Wash the area carefully with soap and water.
> - Apply an ice pack to reduce swelling.
> - Take a pain reliever if necessary.
> - Get medical help immediately if you think you are having an allergic reaction!

1. What can you use to scrape or brush off the stinger? _____

2. Why can't you squeeze the stinger or use tweezers? _____

3. What can you do to reduce swelling? _____

4. What can you do if you think you are having an allergic reaction?

_____

## Sequence the pictures.

Listen. Then number the pictures in the correct order.

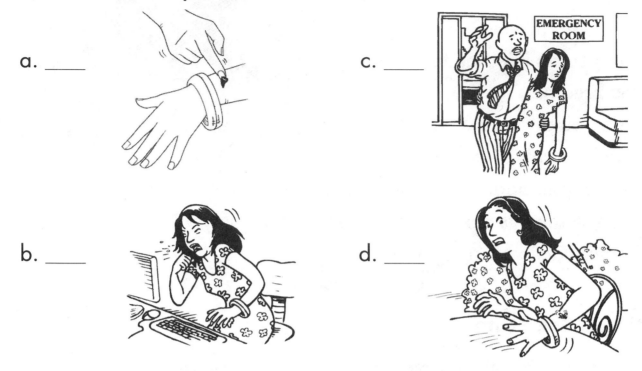

a. ____

c. ____

b. ____

d. ____

## Problem Solving

You don't want to get stung by a bee. What can you do? Check the good ideas. Write other good ideas on the lines.

____ I can wear bright clothing and fragrant perfume.

____ I can stay away from gardens with flowering plants.

____ I can swat at bees to keep them away.

____ I can use unscented soaps and lotions.

____ I can wear light-colored clothing and no perfume.

✓ I can _____

✓ I can _____

## What about you?

Check *Yes* or *No*. Then write the questions and ask your partner.

**Yes**    **No**

\_\_\_\_    \_\_\_\_    1. I wear bright-colored clothing.

*Do you wear bright-colored clothing?* _____

\_\_\_\_    \_\_\_\_    2. I wear perfume or other scented products.

_____

\_\_\_\_    \_\_\_\_    3. I often eat outside.

_____

\_\_\_\_    \_\_\_\_    4. I swat at bees when I see them.

_____

\_\_\_\_    \_\_\_\_    5. I know how to gently scrape or brush off a bee's stinger.

_____

## Topics for Discussion or Writing

1. Did a bee ever sting you? If yes, where were you? Where did it sting you? How did you take care of it?

2. What other insects can sting? What can you do to feel better?

3. Who can help you in a medical emergency at work or at home?

# Health Words

## Lesson 1: Fast Food Decision

**calories** – units that measure the energy a food produces

**carbohydrates** – substances in food that give the body energy; for example, sugars and starches

**cholesterol** – a fatty substance in the body and found in some foods, often linked to heart disease

**diet** – the food that you eat

**fat** – an oily substance in animals and some plants

**grams** – small units of weight, used to measure the amount of fat in a food

**healthy** – good for you

## Lesson 2: Allergic to Penicillin

**allergic** – having or getting a physical reaction from eating, breathing, or touching something that makes you sick

**antibiotic** – medicine that kills bacteria and cures infections

**antihistamine** – drug used for treating an allergy or the conditions that come from an allergic reaction

**bacterial** – caused by a very small living thing that makes people sick

**hives** – itchy red spots on the skin, usually caused by an allergy

**life-threatening** – capable of killing a person

**medical alert card (or bracelet or necklace)** – a piece of cardboard or something to wear that has information about a person's medical condition, including allergies

**penicillin** – a type of antibiotic that kills bacteria and fights disease or infection

**penicillin allergy** – strong reaction to penicillin

**prescription** – a piece of paper that a doctor writes that says what medicine a person needs; an order from a doctor for medicine

**rash** – red spots on the skin

**strep throat** – a bacterial illness that includes a very sore throat

## Lesson 3: Losing Weight

**balanced diet** – a healthy combination of foods from each of the five basic food groups

**blood pressure** – the force of blood when it moves through the body

**cholesterol** – a fatty substance in the body and found in some foods, often linked to heart disease

**diet** – the food that you eat

**energy** – the power to be active

**exercise** – physical activity that increases the health of the body

**healthy** – good for you

**heart disease** – a medical condition in which the heart has difficulty moving blood through the body

**out of breath** – having difficulty getting air in and out of the body

**overweight** – too heavy; weighing more than you should

**physical exam** – a close look at the body by a doctor; a check up

**pounds** – units for measuring weight

**type 2 diabetes** – a serious disease caused by blood glucose (sugar) levels that are too high

## Lesson 4: Seeing Stars

**balance** – the ability to stand and walk without falling

**CAT scan** – a special brain x-ray, sometimes called **CT scan**

**concussion** – an injury to the head and brain caused by hitting your head

**conscious** – awake and able to understand

**injury** – damage to a part of the body

**medication** – another word for medicine; a drug; something you take if you are sick, to make you feel better

**reflexes** – physical reactions that happen without thinking about them

**x-ray** – a photograph that can show the inside of the body, including broken bones

## Lesson 5: Walking and Weights

**bones** – hard parts inside the body

**energy** – the power to be active

**exercise** – physical activity that increases the health of the body

**muscles** – tissues on the bones that produce movement of the bones

**osteoporosis** – a disease that makes your bones break easily

**weights** – heavy objects used for exercise

## Lesson 6: No Room for Wisdom Teeth

**anesthetic** – drug that can prevent feelings of pain

**antibiotic** – medicine that kills bacteria and cures infections

**bleeding** – loss of blood from the body

**diet** – the food that you eat

**extract** – to take out

**impacted** – when there is no room for a tooth to come into the mouth

**infection** – a disease or illness

**medication** – another word for medicine; a drug; something you take if you are sick, to make you feel better

**molars** – teeth at the back of the jaw, used for grinding food

**oral surgeon** – dental professional who can perform oral surgery

**oral surgery** – an operation inside the mouth

**orthodontist** – a dentist who makes teeth straight when they do not come in correctly

**periodontist** – a dentist who treats the gums and diseases of the gums

**swelling** – an area of the body that gets larger

**wisdom teeth** – the third molars; the last teeth on each side at the back of the mouth

## Lesson 7: The Chicken Casserole

**bacteria** – very small living things that cause illness; germs

**diarrhea** – a condition involving frequent and watery bowel movements

**food poisoning** – stomach illness that is caused by eating food that contains harmful bacteria

**medication** – another word for medicine; a drug; something you take if you are sick, to make you feel better

**vomit** – to bring food up from the stomach

## Lesson 8: Coughing and Sneezing

**cold** – a viral infection with symptoms like coughing, sneezing, headaches, and nasal congestion

**coughing** – forcing air and other substances from your mouth loudly

**cure** – to make a person healthy with a medicine or treatment

**dizziness** – a feeling as if you are going to fall, often with a feeling that things are moving around you

**drowsiness** – tiredness or sleepiness

**germs** – small things that can cause illness

**medication** – another word for medicine; a drug; something you take if you are sick, to make you feel better

**pharmacy** – drugstore; a store or an area in a store where you buy medications

**sneezing** – letting air come out of the mouth and nose suddenly and with force

**virus** – a very small living thing that causes a disease; also the disease that it causes

**warning** – advice to be careful about something; information about a possible danger

## Lesson 9: A Busy Nurse-Practitioner

**antibiotic-resistant** – when bacteria (germs) are harder to kill with antibiotics

**antibiotics** – medicine that kills bacteria and cures infections

**bacteria** – very small living things that cause illness

**bacterial infection** – a disease or illness caused by bacteria

**cough** – condition of forcing air and other substances from your mouth loudly

**diagnose** – to identify an illness or find out what is making a person sick

**fever** – a high body temperature

**flu** – an illness like a serious cold, caused by a virus; short form for *influenza*

**nurse-practitioner** – a nurse who can diagnose and treat minor illnesses

**otoscope** – instrument for examining the ear

**patients** – people having medical treatment

**pharmacy** – drugstore; a store or an area in a store where you buy medications

**symptoms** – signs of an illness

**virus** – a very small living thing that causes a disease; also the disease that it causes

## Lesson 10: Tonsils Out

**infection** – a disease or illness

**operation** – a medical procedure to repair or remove a part of the body

**snores** – breathes loudly while sleeping

**swallowing** – moving liquids or solids from the mouth down the throat

**throat** – the part of the body at the back of the mouth; the inside of the neck

**tonsillectomy** – an operation to take out the tonsils

**tonsillitis** – a throat infection involving the tonsils

**tonsils** – two small organs, one at each side of the back of the throat

## Lesson 11: Missing a Vaccine

**clinic** – a place to get medical treatment for problems that do not require visits to the hospital

**dose** – a measured quantity of a vaccine or medication

**hepatitis B** – a disease caused by a virus that attacks the liver

**immunization** – act of protecting someone from a disease by giving that person a vaccine

**immunization records** – documents showing dates of vaccines

**liver** – organ in the body that cleans the blood

**measles** – a viral disease that causes red spots on the body

**polio** – a serious disease that often causes paralysis, or the inability to move your muscles

**school nurse** – medical professional working at a school site

**vaccine** – medicine that prevents disease

**virus** – a very small living thing that causes a disease; also the disease that it causes

## Lesson 12: Type 2 Diabetes

**calorie** – a unit that measures the energy a food produces

**diet** – the food that you eat

**energy** – the power to be active

**exercise** – physical activity

**glucose** – a sugar that your body needs

**lab test** – a study of a sample of body tissue or fluid, performed in a laboratory to diagnose illness

**medication** – another word for medicine; a drug; something you take if you are sick, to make you feel better

**overweight** – too heavy; weighing more than you should

**thirsty** – feeling the need to drink something

**type 2 diabetes** – a disease caused by blood glucose levels that are too high

**urinates** – makes liquid waste flow from the body

## Lesson 13: Protect Your Skin from the Sun

**basal cell carcinoma** – the most common skin cancer

**biopsy** – the removal of body tissue for laboratory examination

**bump** – a raised area on a surface

**cancer** – a serious disease, in which certain cells in the body grow much faster than they should

**dermatologist** – a doctor for the skin

**microscope** – a device that makes small objects appear larger

**sunscreen** – a cream or other product that prevents your skin from burning in the sun

**treat** – to give medical help

## Lesson 14: The Bee Sting

**allergic reaction** – physical symptoms from eating, breathing, or touching something that makes you sick

**coughing** – forcing air and other substances from your mouth loudly

**die** – to no longer live

**emergency room** – area in hospital for immediate help

**fingernail** – hard, flat covering at the end of your finger

**injection** – a shot of medicine from a syringe, or needle

**itch** – to feel the need to scratch your skin or another body part

**medication** – another word for medicine; a drug; something you take if you are sick, to make you feel better

**rash** – red spots on the skin

**sneeze** – to let air come out of the mouth and nose suddenly and with force

**stinger** – sharp part of a bee that injects poison

**swelling** – an area of the body that gets larger

**venom** – poison from certain snakes and insects

# Listening Exercise Prompts

## Lesson 2

### Sequence the pictures. (p. 14)

1. Sami sees a terrible rash on his body.
2. The doctor looks carefully at Sami's rash in the examining room.
3. The doctor writes a prescription for another antibiotic.
4. The doctor tells Sami to carry an alert card in his wallet.

## Lesson 3

### Write the number of pounds you hear. (p. 20)

1. Oh, no. I'm 50 pounds heavier than I was in high school.
2. The doctor wants me to lose 40 pounds.
3. Congratulations! You're 25 pounds lighter.
4. Walking daily has helped me lose 15 pounds.
5. She's on a diet. She wants to lose 30 pounds.
6. John gets out of breath easily. He is 60 pounds overweight.
7. You have gained 45 pounds in the last three years.
8. I am 10 pounds heavier than I was last year.
9. I want to lose 5 pounds this month.
10. Diet and exercise can help you lose 70 pounds.

## Lesson 5

### Write the distance you hear. (p. 32)

1. The doctor wants me to walk one mile a day.
2. The bank is only a half mile from here.
3. Do you think we can walk three-quarters of a mile?
4. She jogs three miles a day.
5. The distance to school is about two and a half miles.
6. Right now she can only walk about one-quarter of a mile.
7. The supermarket is two miles from her home.
8. He lives one and a quarter miles from his sister.
9. Every Saturday I jog four miles.
10. Let's walk there. It's only one and a half miles.

11. The park is three and a quarter miles from here.
12. I can walk two and a quarter miles now.

## Lesson 7

### Sequence the pictures. (p. 44)

1. Andre finds a shallow container.
2. He covers it with a lid that fits tightly.
3. He writes the date on the container.
4. He checks that the temperature inside the refrigerator is 40 degrees Fahrenheit.

## Lesson 9

### Sequence the pictures. (p. 56)

1. Today Mara is talking on the phone to Mr. Avila.
2. Never take antibiotics when you don't need them.
3. Mrs. Tweed has a cough. Antibiotics can't help her.
4. Mara looks in Rose's ear with an otoscope.

## Lesson 11

### Sequence the pictures. (p. 68)

1. Liem is registering Tai for the sixth grade.
2. The nurse is checking immunization records.
3. The school nurse gives Liem some information from the Public Health Department.
4. Tai gets his third dose of the hepatitis B vaccine.

## Lesson 12

### Sequence the pictures. (p. 74)

1. Mateo eats too many high-calorie foods.
2. Lately Mateo feels thirsty all the time.
3. He urinates often.
4. He doesn't have a lot of energy.

## Lesson 14

### Sequence the pictures. (p. 86)

1. A bee stings Elena's arm.
2. She brushes off the stinger with her fingernail.
3. Soon Elena starts coughing.
4. Her co-worker takes her to the hospital emergency room.

# Answer Key

## Lesson 1

**Answer the questions. (p. 5)**

1. almost every day
2. fast food
3. Oscar's co-worker
4. It's bad for you.
5. more than 500
6. 25
7. to the Greenhouse Café
8. a spinach salad and whole-grain bread
9. delicious
10. an extra-large double-chocolate shake

**Which category is it? (p. 6)**

*Nutrition Factors*

1. calories
2. carbohydrates
3. cholesterol
4. fat grams

*Fast Food*

1. cheeseburger
2. fried chicken
3. hot dog
4. pizza

*Words that Describe Food*

1. delicious
2. greasy
3. healthy
4. heavy

**Matching: Definitions (p. 6)**

1. f
2. b
3. a
4. e
5. c
6. d

**Fast Food Menu (p. 7)**

1. 37
2. 450
3. quarter-pound cheeseburger
4. large slice of pizza
5. large slice of pizza

**Sequence the story. (p. 8)**

4, 6, 2, 5, 1, 3

## Lesson 2

**Answer the questions. (p. 11)**

1. for strep throat
2. all over his back, chest, arms, and stomach
3. right away
4. stop taking the penicillin
5. hives
6. He is allergic to penicillin.
7. six more days
8. another antibiotic
9. an antihistamine
10. a penicillin allergy

**Check the sentence that means the same. (p. 12)**

1. a
2. b
3. b
4. b
5. a
6. a

**Medical Alert Card (p. 13)**

1. Mansour
2. 1947 Vista Grande Avenue
3. Mark Wilkins
4. Penicillin
5. O+

**Sequence the pictures. (p. 14)**

a. 3
b. 4
c. 1
d. 2

## Lesson 3

**Answer the questions. (p. 17)**

1. 40 years old
2. 50 pounds
3. He doesn't look healthy, and he doesn't feel healthy.
4. lose weight
5. serious health problems, such as heart disease, type 2 diabetes, high cholesterol, and high blood pressure
6. slowly and sensibly
7. He walks daily, uses the stairs, and eats a balanced diet.
8. He doesn't fry his food, and he bakes, broils, and steams when he cooks.
9. after nine months
10. 50 pounds

**Which category is it? (p. 18)**

*Health Problems*

1. heart disease
2. high blood pressure
3. high cholesterol
4. type 2 diabetes

*Ways to Cook*

1. bake
2. broil
3. fry
4. steam

*Exercise*

1. biking
2. climbing stairs
3. swimming
4. walking

**Matching: Opposites (p. 18)**

1. f
2. c
3. b
4. a
5. d
6. g
7. e

**Healthy Cooking (p. 19)**
1. lose weight
2. flavor and nutrients
3. extra fat and sodium
4. fruit juice, vegetable juice
5. reduce fat and calories

**Write the number of pounds you hear. (p. 20)**

| | | | |
|---|---|---|---|
| 1. 50 | 4. 15 | 7. 45 | 9. 5 |
| 2. 40 | 5. 30 | 8. 10 | 10. 70 |
| 3. 25 | 6. 60 | | |

## Lesson 4

**Answer the questions. (p. 23)**
1. cleaning her house
2. on a high shelf in her living room
3. a wobbly, old chair
4. backwards
5. her head
6. her husband
7. to the hospital
8. a CAT scan
9. a concussion
10. rest

**Check the sentence that means the same. (p. 24)**

| | | |
|---|---|---|
| 1. b | 3. b | 5. b |
| 2. a | 4. b | 6. a |

**Care for Concussion (p. 25)**
1. wake her at least once during the night and contact the doctor if Lucy is difficult to wake or confused
2. any vomiting
3. acetaminophen or other aspirin-free medication for headaches
4. rest
5. when the pain and other symptoms are gone

**Sequence the story. (p. 26)**
3, 6, 5, 1, 4, 2

## Lesson 5

**Answer the questions. (p. 29)**
1. 71
2. her dog, Coco
3. a neighbor
4. she has some back pain
5. makes muscles stronger and slows the progress of osteoporosis

6. walking and using weights
7. a quarter mile
8. one mile
9. three times a week
10. good walking shoes and hand weights

**Check the sentence that means the same. (p. 30)**

| | | |
|---|---|---|
| 1. b | 3. a | 5. a |
| 2. a | 4. b | 6. a |

**Exercise for Seniors (p. 31)**
1. a mile
2. legs, hips, lower spine
3. arms and upper spine
4. a disease that makes your bones break easily

**Write the distance you hear. (p. 32)**

| | | |
|---|---|---|
| 1. 1 mile | 5. 2½ miles | 9. 4 miles |
| 2. ½ mile | 6. ¼ mile | 10. 1½ miles |
| 3. ¾ mile | 7. 2 miles | 11. 3¼ miles |
| 4. 3 miles | 8. 1¼ miles | 12. 2¼ miles |

## Lesson 6

**Answer the questions. (p. 35)**
1. 20 years old
2. They have to be taken out.
3. They are impacted.
4. They can hurt her other teeth.
5. to an oral surgeon
6. an anesthetic
7. four
8. some bleeding and swelling
9. to prevent infection
10. in one week

**Which category is it? (p. 36)**
*Dental Professionals*

| | |
|---|---|
| 1. dentist | 3. orthodontist |
| 2. oral surgeon | 4. periodontist |

*Problems after Surgery*

| | |
|---|---|
| 1. bleeding | 3. pain |
| 2. infection | 4. swelling |

*Things Ling Needs*

| | |
|---|---|
| 1. anesthetic | 3. pain medication |
| 2. antibiotics | 4. special diet |

**Matching: Definitions (p. 36)**

| | | |
|---|---|---|
| 1. e | 3. b | 5. a |
| 2. d | 4. f | 6. c |

**Swelling after Oral Surgery (p. 37)**

1. swelling, for two or three days
2. 24 hours
3. pillows
4. fever or a bad taste in your mouth

**Sequence the story. (p. 38)**

4, 3, 6, 1, 5, 2

## Lesson 7

**Answer the questions. (p. 41)**

1. chicken casserole
2. in the refrigerator
3. only 30 minutes ago
4. bacteria
5. a shallow container
6. a lid that fits tightly
7. the date
8. 40 degrees Fahrenheit
9. four days later
10. in the trash

**Check the sentence that means the same. (p. 42)**

1. b        3. a        5. b
2. a        4. b        6. a

**Food Poisoning Prevention (p. 43)**

1. any food that is not refrigerated within two hours
2. no higher than 40 degrees Fahrenheit
3. no
4. bacteria
5. no more than four days

**Sequence the pictures. (p. 44)**

a. 3        b. 4        c. 1        d. 2

## Lesson 8

**Answer the questions. (p. 47)**

1. taxi driver
2. ten-hour shifts, six day a week
3. to support his family
4. not well; he has a bad cold, and he's coughing and sneezing.
5. turn their heads away from him
6. "Thanks for spreading your germs. No tip for you!"
7. some cold medicine

8. the label
9. "This medication may cause dizziness or drowsiness. Be careful when driving or operating machinery."
10. He can't take the medicines and drive a taxi. He needs to take some time off to get better.

**Check the sentence that means the same. (p. 48)**

1. b        3. a        5. a
2. b        4. b        6. a

**Cold Medicine (p. 49)**

1. Cold-Away
2. sneezing and coughing
3. dizzy or drowsy
4. alcoholic drinks
5. when driving a motor vehicle or operating machinery
6. no, because he needs to drive his taxi

**Sequence the story. (p. 50)**

3, 1, 5, 6, 4, 2

## Lesson 9

**Answer the questions. (p. 53)**

1. nurse-practitioner
2. in a busy doctor's office
3. antibiotics
4. They become antibiotic-resistant, so they don't work when you really need them.
5. antibiotics
6. "Antibiotics can't help you."
7. She has a fever, and her ear hurts.
8. an otoscope
9. a bacterial infection
10. antibiotics

**Check the sentence that means the same. (p. 54)**

1. a        3. b        5. a
2. b        4. a        6. a

**Using Antibiotics (p. 55)**

1. bacterial infections
2. Bacteria become antibiotic-resistant.
3. yes
4. no

**Sequence the pictures. (p. 56)**

a. 3        b. 2        c. 1        d. 4

# Lesson 10
## Answer the questions. (p. 59)
1. seven years old
2. tonsillitis
3. snores loudly
4. exhausted
5. to an ear, nose, and throat doctor
6. an operation to take out her tonsils
7. a tonsillectomy
8. only about 20 minutes
9. food that is soft on her throat, such as ice pops, gelatin, ice cream, and soup
10. Nika's father

## Which category is it? (p. 60)
### Parts of the Body
1. ears
2. neck
3. nose
4. throat

### Soft Foods
1. gelatin
2. ice cream
3. ice pops
4. soup

### Activities Affected by Tonsillitis
1. breathing
2. drinking
3. eating
4. swallowing

## Matching: Definitions (p. 60)
1. f
2. d
3. a
4. c
5. e
6. b

## Preparing for a Tonsillectomy (p. 61)
1. anything to eat or drink
2. about 20 minutes
3. fluids
4. on the day of the operation
5. about two weeks

## Sequence the story. (p. 62)
2, 5, 4, 6, 1, 3

# Lesson 11
## Answer the questions. (p. 65)
1. in the office of Big Rock Middle School
2. sixth grade
3. many forms
4. the school nurse
5. his third dose of the hepatitis B vaccine
6. a serious disease caused by a virus that attacks the liver
7. some information from the Public Health Department
8. every Friday
9. his third dose of the hepatitis B vaccine
10. on Monday

## Which category is it? (p. 66)
### Things Necessary for School
1. birth certificate
2. immunization record
3. proof of home address
4. school records

### Places to Get Immunizations
1. community clinic
2. doctor's office
3. hospital
4. mobile clinic

### Serious Diseases
1. hepatitis B
2. measles
3. polio
4. tuberculosis

## Matching: Definitions (p. 66)
1. b
2. c
3. d
4. f
5. e
6. a

## Immunization Information (p. 67)
1. every Friday
2. yes
3. $10
4. 8:00 to 11:00 A.M. and 1:00 to 4:00 P.M.

## Sequence the pictures. (p. 68)
a. 3
b. 4
c. 2
d. 1

# Lesson 12
## Answer the questions. (p. 71)
1. 12 years old
2. too many high-calorie foods and a lot of sugary sodas
3. because Mateo feels thirsty all the time, urinates often, and doesn't have a lot of energy
4. several lab tests
5. type 2 diabetes
6. the blood glucose level
7. his blood glucose levels
8. exercise, medication, and diet
9. high-calorie foods and sodas
10. a soda

**Check the sentence that means the same. (p. 72)**

1. b      3. a      5. b
2. a      4. a      6. b

**Diabetes Diet (p. 73)**

1. blood glucose levels
2. fruit, vegetables, whole grains; because the body breaks them down slowly
3. processed foods; because the body breaks them down quickly
4. water

**Sequence the pictures. (p. 74)**

a. 4      b. 1      c. 2      d. 3

## Lesson 13

**Answer the questions. (p. 77)**

1. in Florida
2. to go to the beach and sit in the sun for hours
3. a hat or sunscreen
4. a bump
5. a doctor for the skin, called a dermatologist
6. a biopsy
7. a basal cell carcinoma
8. in her office
9. to avoid the sun between 10 A.M. and 4 P.M., to wear a long-sleeved shirt and hat when he is outdoors, to always use sunscreen, and to check his skin for signs of skin cancer
10. every month

**Check the sentence that means the same. (p. 78)**

1. b      3. b      5. a
2. a      4. b      6. a

**Sun Protection Advice (p. 79)**

1. between 10 A.M. and 4 P.M.
2. a long-sleeved shirt, a wide-brimmed hat, and UV-blocking sunglasses
3. SPF 15 or higher
4. every month
5. as early as possible

**Sequence the story. (p. 80)**

3, 5, 2, 1, 6, 4

## Lesson 14

**Answer the questions. (p. 83)**

1. a bright, flowery dress and a fragrant perfume
2. in a little garden outside her office
3. a peanut butter and jelly sandwich
4. on her arm
5. washes the bee sting with soap and water
6. She starts coughing, begins to sneeze and itch, and gets a rash.
7. to the hospital emergency room
8. an injection and other medication
9. medication for her allergy to bee stings
10. light-colored clothing and no perfume

**Which category is it? (p. 84)**

*Things that Attract Bees*

1. bright colors      3. garden
2. food      4. perfume

*Signs of Allergic Reactions*

1. cough      3. rash
2. itch      4. sneeze

*Things to Help Bee Stings*

1. icepack      3. soap
2. pain reliever      4. water

**Matching**

1. d      3. f      5. b      7. a
2. c      4. g      6. e

**Treating a Bee Sting (p. 85)**

1. gauze or a straight-edged object
2. because you can cause more venom to go into the skin
3. apply an ice pack
4. get medical help immediately

**Sequence the pictures. (p. 86)**

a. 2      b. 3      c. 4      d. 1